# BITCOIN: What are the Kids up to NOW?

*First steps in the cryptocurrency world*

NATHANIEL ROLLINS

Copyright © 2018 Nathaniel Rollins

All rights reserved.

ISBN: 9781729408810

# DEDICATION

To my dear friend Jeff.

# CONTENTS

| | | |
|---|---|---|
| 1 | Bitcoin: What are the Kids up to Now? | 1 |
| 2 | Beyond belief: The Blockchain. | 3 |
| 3 | What Is A Bitcoin Address? | 5 |
| 4 | Bitcoin Wallet. | 7 |
| 5 | Is Bitcoin Free to Use? | 8 |
| 6 | What happens if you forget to include a fee or include one that is too low? | 10 |
| 7 | Why Bitcoin is Special. | 11 |
| 8 | Who Controls Bitcoin? | 14 |
| 9 | Can anyone mine and Is it profitable? | 18 |
| 10 | So You Want to get Your Digital Hands on Some Juicy Bitcoin... | 19 |
| 11 | Exchanging Bitcoin. | 22 |
| 12 | How Not to Obtain Bitcoin! | 24 |
| 13 | Investing in Bitcoin. | 25 |
| 14 | Bitcoin Security | 27 |
| 15 | Possible Threats. | 28 |
| 16 | Challenges for Bitcoins Longevity and Mainstream Appeal.Mainstream Appeal | 36 |
| 17 | Summary | 40 |

NATHANIEL ROLLINS

# 1 BITCOIN: WHAT ARE THE KIDS UP TO NOW?

Bitcoin and other cryptocurrencies are a way to send, receive, and store value, like money, without Central Banks, payment processors, or other third parties.

Bitcoin (BTC) is a currency. You want something you can buy it with Bitcoin, provided the seller also believes in the value of the cryptocurrency.

We will explore some other crazy differences between Bitcoin and conventional fiat currencies throughout the book, but I do want to touch on the idea of belief and currency because that is an understandable concern people have when they hear about Bitcoin. "What in the wide world of sports makes it valuable? Belief? Thanks but no thanks. I will stick to (fill in fiat currency here)."

"Fiat money is currency that a government has declared to be legal tender, but it is not backed by a physical commodity. The value of fiat money is derived from the relationship between supply and demand rather than the value of the material that the money is made of." https://www.investopedia.com/terms/f/fiatmoney.asp

You want to talk about belief? Holy cow! Ask the

citizenry in Greece how belief in fiat currencies works.

In 2012 the Republic of Cyprus underwent a serious financial crisis when it could no longer repay its debts. Cyprus' solution included temporarily freezing their citizens' access to "their" money in banks, followed by a one-time levy on bank accounts with balances over a certain amount. In other words, they took money out of their citizens' bank accounts.

This is not science fiction, ancient history or some crackheads, alleyway mutterings; this actually happened less than a decade ago. What would prevent it from happening elsewhere? The bank bailout was a pretty nifty trick. The point is, the money you have in the bank is not yours. Bitcoin, if you have any, is yours. Bitcoin that is in your "wallet" can only be accessed by you.

# 2 BEYOND BELIEF: THE BLOCKCHAIN.

Bitcoin is a currency and a method of banking to track ownership of wealth like a bank but instead of updating a globally distributed ledger of accounts tied to people and fiat currencies Bitcoin ties the wealth that is anchored to the Blockchain.

Traditional debt based banks track how much money you have. They keep the ledger. When you buy something with your debit/credit card, your bank removes the same amount from their ledger and the merchant's bank adds the money to theirs. Easy enough.

Now imagine that instead of multiple banks with multiple ledgers, there was only one "bank", known as the Bitcoin Blockchain, with one, worldwide ledger. When you buy something with Bitcoin, the one bank that both you and the merchant share updates its one ledger, showing that ten dollars have changed ownership from you to the merchant. This "bank" is a network of computers connected to internet connecting the Blockchain. Instead of Dollars or Euros, values in the blockchain or ledger are called bitcoins.

The name comes from the way it is maintained. Transactions are not written individually, but in blocks- or collections of many transactions. The Bitcoin blockchain is:

- Complete. It contains every Bitcoin transaction ever made.
- Nearly Unchangeable. While not "impossible", it is extremely difficult to modify a Bitcoin transaction once it has been written to the ledger. Not only that, but every block of transactions makes it more difficult to change the preceding blocks. If a transaction has over six blocks written on top of it, it is essentially unchangeable.

Public and So Private. The Blockchain is not secret; anyone can view it and its contents online. Does this mean that people can view your Bitcoin transactions? Yes. You can look up any Bitcoin transaction and see related transactions which came before and after it. However, the only information in the ledger are Bitcoin addresses (consider them to be like account numbers for now), transaction IDs, timestamps and amounts. You do not see names or items purchased. You do not see information that would allow you to assume someone's identity or conduct transactions using their money. The only information available is a record of BTC moving from one set of addresses to another.

Distributed. The Bitcoin ledger has thousands of identical copies in the Bitcoin network....

# 3 WHAT IS A BITCOIN ADDRESS?

Bitcoin is held in addresses, and transactions on the public ledger show BTC moving from one or more source addresses to one or more destination addresses. At first glance, each Bitcoin address seems like random numbers and letters in both upper and lowercase. You don't need to memorize, recognize, or type these addresses to send bitcoin to someone. You will either click a link that has the recipient's Bitcoin address (and sometimes the amount of BTC) embedded in it, scan a code that contains the destination address, or copy/paste the address into your Bitcoin wallet from an email, website, or other source.

If you ever find yourself manually typing a Bitcoin address into something... STOP. Something is wrong.

One comparison you will hear often is that a Bitcoin address is like a bank account number. I prefer to compare Bitcoin addresses to reloadable gift cards. Each card has its own number, and none of the "cards" has your name attached to it.

You load a card with dollars and you spend it wherever the card is accepted. Once the balance reaches zero, you can either load that same card with more money and keep using it, or you can buy a new gift card with a different number and use that one instead. Now imagine you had a wallet full of these debit cards, and the ability to transfer money between them.

You fancy a little pick-me-up and head to the coffee shop, purchasing your little treat using Card #1. The drink is $2.50, and the card has $25.00 on it. The remaining balance, $22.50, moves to Card #2. Later, you use Card #2 to buy a Justin B. t shirt for $15.00. The remaining $7.50 is now on Card #3. This chain of transactions continues until your balance reaches zero. This is how you use Bitcoin. Each "card" is a Bitcoin address, and you manage the addresses with a Bitcoin wallet that allows you to make transactions and shift balances between them. Depending on the wallet, leftover funds from a transaction or the change, will return to the original Bitcoin address or be sent to a new address that is generated automatically.

# 4 BITCOIN WALLET.

There are plenty of Bitcoin wallets to choose from. Some platforms such as Android have more choices than others, but wallets for other types of smartphones have nearly identical feature sets. Desktop wallets have also offer additional features but tend not to be as user-friendly.

A mobile wallet is a good start for beginners. Make sure the wallet you choose is storing data and performing the transactions on your device, not just serving as a front-end to a wallet service based in the cloud. If you can go to a website and type a username and password to access your BTC outside of the app... don't use that service. Avoid web-based wallets.

# 5 IS BITCOIN FREE TO USE?

Hypothetically yes but mostly no. There are two fees that most users will encounter when using Bitcoin. The first are the fees that exchanges charge to convert dollars to bitcoin. If you are sending BTC to someone who will be converting it to USD or some other currency, you should include enough extra to cover any conversion fees.

Keeping track of transactions to a ledger is easy. Writing blocks of transactions to a distributed public ledger that prevents them from being manipulated is more difficult. This is why those performing this vital service for the Bitcoin network expect to be compensated. That is where transaction fees come in.

Fees are tied to how complex your transaction is. Throughout Bitcoin's history, recommended transaction fees have ranged from fractions of a cent to just over a dollar per transaction. Note the use of the word "recommended". The Bitcoin network does not force you to include a minimum fee. If your wallet software allows it, you can perform transactions with no fee at all. If you do this, your transaction may take days or weeks to be written if it is written at all.

As the Bitcoin network increases in size, miners will

have an increasing incentive to ignore transactions that do not include adequate fees. One of your friend's BTC transaction might be confirmed within an hour after paying just a $.50 fee, while the transaction fee you included of $1.50 is confirmed in ten minutes. There is not an exact fee-to-minutes guide you can refer to but good Bitcoin wallets will make suggestions of fee amounts for "low priority" or "high priority" transactions. You should look for and follow those suggestions. It is also helpful to verify the transaction includes an adequate fee. Do this by viewing the transaction in your BTC wallet..

# 6 WHAT HAPPENS IF YOU FORGET TO INCLUDE A FEE OR INCLUDE ONE THAT IS TOO LOW?

It is more than likely that your transaction will still be confirmed, but it will take longer. Instead of minutes, verification of the transaction could languish in the backlog for up to fourteen days. At that point the system will cancel the transaction and return the BTC to you. If you are on the receiving end of transactions you should wait for the network confirmation before rendering goods or services.

There are ways to increase the fee after it is sent but these methods are neither, free, guaranteed, or easy.

Transaction accelerator services will include your transaction into the next block they write into the public ledger. These services are a pain in the eyelashes so better to avoid the hassle by including the fees up front.

# 7 WHY BITCOIN IS SPECIAL.

**Bitcoin is Non-reversible.** Unlike credit card transactions and PayPal, Bitcoin transactions are non-reversible. Once a Bitcoin transaction has been confirmed, the BTC has permanently changed hands. Neither the sender nor any 3rd party can undo the transaction. It is equivalent to handing someone cash. This is super awesome for merchants who no longer have to worry about chargebacks.

**Bitcoin has relatively low fees.** While the fee for sending bitcoin can vary greatly, it is determined by how complex the transaction is and how soon you want the transaction to be written to the ledger. It is NOT determined by distance, the number of borders that must be crossed, or the amount of BTC involved. Sending $100 worth of BTC to someone across the street costs the same as sending $100,000 to someone on the other side of the globe. However, if you want the transaction confirmed as quickly as possible, expect to pay a bit more.

**Bitcoin has no mandatory 3rd Parties.** If you send someone money through traditional means, you do so with the involvement of both yours and the recipient's bank, plus the added scrutiny of the government.

When you buy something with a credit card, both the store's bank and payment processor are involved in the transaction. These 3rd parties are mostly beneficial to both parties conducting trade Third parties are can also be a liability. What if things go wonky? Maybe the store's credit card processor gets hacked or Visa and Mastercard stop doing business with you due to political pressure? That is what happened to Wikimedia in 2014. PayPal has also been known to also throw their weight around on behalf of interested parties. Perhaps you have a misunderstanding with the IRS, and they freeze your bank account while they clear things up? These things do happen and can be extremely disruptive.

This interference is impossible when dealing with Bitcoin. Many merchants do however willingly use a Bitcoin third party payment processor like BitPay or Coinbase for ease of use.

**Bitcoin is finite.** The number of bitcoins is capped at 21 million. Once that last bitcoin is created/mined NO ONE can create more. This finite supply is the reason bitcoin is un-inflatable.

Conversely, the potential number of US dollars is infinite. Every year the government creates more money, (not to be confused with wealth), and in doing so makes the existing dollars less valuable. This is why your grandpapa tells all those stories about a soda pop costing a nickel, and why the money you put in your bank account today will not buy as much when you are telling your grandkids about how much you used to pay for a soda pop. Bitcoin doesn't have an inflationary issue but in terms of USD., the value of bitcoin has fluctuated quite dramatically. However, this fluctuation is not due to the production of more currency.

**Bitcoin is divisible.** The smallest unit of US currency is the penny, or $0.01 USD. The smallest unit of BTC is the satoshi, or 0.00000001 BTC. Bitcoin is divisible up to 8 decimal places, which, in theory, allows it to be used for very small transactions known as "micro-payments." A micro-payment system might allow viewers to pay for videos by the minute, or allow you to go back to the counter because you forgot to buy an extra side of ranch dressing for your sweet potato fries.

However, rising transaction fees make BTC less suitable for small transactions. Proposed changes to the Bitcoin protocol may well return fees to a level low enough renew interest in micropayments.

While 8 decimal places are the CURRENT limit of divisibility it can be increased and ongoing discussions on possible solutions like; scripting, multi-signature addresses, and digital autonomous corporations are far beyond what is appropriate for an introductory text. The only thing a new or potential Bitcoin user should know about them is that Bitcoin has more potential than what you've read so far. The Bitcoin protocol can do some strange, interesting, and very useful things. These things have little impact on how you might use Bitcoin as a new user but the possibilities are important to understand.

# 8 WHO CONTROLS BITCOIN?

Bitcoin is not a product of any government, corporation, or organization. It does not have a President, CEO, or Board of Directors. Bitcoin is structured in a way that no individual or singular group can change how it works.

Bitcoin is updated often, but the changes are agreed upon by multiple parties, each acting as much in their own interests as the interests of the Bitcoin economy. None of these parties "control" Bitcoin on their own, but the evolution of the Bitcoin protocol occurs through their interaction:

**Developers.** Bitcoin is implemented in software, so the developers are in control, right? If someone wanted to introduce a change to Bitcoin, could they not just influence one of the Bitcoin developers to add that change to some new version of Bitcoin? They could. But the code that runs Bitcoin, much like the distributed ledger of transactions, is public. Interested parties are constantly looking at the code and all the changes made to it. Any sneaky-snake change someone tried to make almost certainly would not make it out of code review and would certainly be discovered in the testing phase that all new versions of the software undergo prior to release. But suppose someone influenced ALL of the developers? Could they get together and change the maximum number of bitcoins to 50 million, for instance? If they did, they'd have to answer to...

**The Network.** Miners aren't the only people essential to the network. Every person running properly configured Bitcoin software on their computer is part of the network. They don't write transactions to the ledger, but they do communicate with one another to propagate those transactions across the Bitcoin network. If you buy an item online with bitcoin, your transaction will be visible on the Bitcoin network within seconds of you hitting send, even though the transaction has not yet been written to the ledger. The other non-mining machines on the network make that happen. However, just like miners, these users have to update their software in order for new versions of Bitcoin to take hold. Just like miners, they can choose to run old or alternative versions of the software if they don't like what the the changes made by developers.

**End Users.** Never underestimate the power of the end user. It is the people making transactions that give Bitcoin its value. No entity can force you to use a specific version of Bitcoin or to use Bitcoin at all. The end users can and will abandon any "new" version of Bitcoin that does not have their best interests at heart. This is the ultimate veto, and developers and miners know it.

Unfortunately, as the user base grows, the level of involvement of the average user is dropping. Most users don't care what the developers and miners are arguing about on a weekly basis... nor should they. The veto power of the end user will probably be wielded by the people who make the Bitcoin wallets, who can choose to implement or ignore changes to the protocol, within reason.

Many changes to Bitcoin is an epic struggle among these powerful parties. Most changes to the Bitcoin protocol are minor, beneficial and noncontroversial. But when there are wildly different opinions on what effects a change might have, the process can be prolonged and extremely contentious. These are a non issue for people casually using BTC, but investors and traders need to stay informed as part of their due diligence.

**Miners.** Miners run the machines that write the transactions to the public ledger. They get paid from the fees that users include in their transactions. If a new version of Bitcoin is released, miners must update the software on their machines in order for the changes to be implemented. Or they can just ignore it. If miners feel that the "new version" of Bitcoin will harm their business or negatively affect the price of BTC, they can reject it by simply not running it. Miners have different ideas about what is and is not good for Bitcoin so some will run the new code while others may not. The code that ends up with the most computing power behind it "wins". If there is no clear winner, there may be two competing versions of Bitcoin existing side-by-side for a time.

**Bitcoin Mining.**

Every connected computer to the Bitcoin network is a node. Nodes relay transactions, hold a full copy of the public ledger, and can also be used as Bitcoin wallets. But not all nodes are equal.

Some members of the network are engaged in the crucial task of "confirming" or

writing transactions to the ledger. These special nodes are called Miners. The nature of the work they are performing is both complex and difficult... so much so that it requires specialized hardware to perform efficiently. However, these miners aren't performing this work out of the goodness of their hearts. The Bitcoin network compensates them in two ways for every block of transactions they write to the ledger:

- They receive the transaction fees contained in that block of transactions
- They receive a mining reward of 25 BTC. This

amount goes down every few years, and will eventually reach zero, forcing miners to rely solely on transaction fees for income.

Miners are competing with one another to confirm the next block of transactions. Since mining is so difficult, most miners join "pools" that combine their computing power and split any rewards they earn.

# 9 CAN ANYONE MINE AND IS IT PROFITABLE?

Technically, anyone can mine. There is nothing stopping you from installing the Bitcoin software on your PC and joining the network as a miner. However, the likelihood of you mining a block and receiving the associated rewards is vanishingly small. You'd essentially be wasting your time and electricity.

To be honest. Mining for a couple of nice folks like us, does not matter too much. Just know that a network of computers compute these crazy mathematical whatnots called blocks that add to the blockchain. In the early days, bitcoin mining could be done with a normal PC. Now, it is a highly sophisticated proposition and if you don't have access to serious start-up capital don't even think about it. It is an industry now.

# 10 SO YOU WANT TO GET YOUR DIGITAL HANDS ON SOME JUICY BITCOIN...

Online Bitcoin Exchanges are the most straightforward way to purchase BTC. Exchanges accept deposits of USD, typically from a bank account or credit card, and exchange those dollars for an equivalent amount of BTC. The process is easy enough but there are a few things new users should keep in mind.

Online exchanges will request your personal information before they will work with you. You must provide a copy of a driver's license or similar ID and perhaps answer questions about the source of your funds. This is a federal requirement that anyone who has opened a bank or brokerage account should be familiar with. Those who are unfamiliar may consider this to be an invasion of privacy or balk at providing personal identifying information over the internet. Also note that the exchange will take time to process the information you give them, and you will have restricted or no access to their services while they do so.

Do not expect to open an account with an online

exchange and immediately buy/sell massive amounts of BTC. If you need to get your hands on some bitcoin immediately, consider one of the other methods.

In the past, some online exchanges (Coinbase) have tracked the movement of the bitcoin that their customers bought. Recall that the Bitcoin ledger is public, and the exchange knows what address it sent the BTC to. Customers who used their newly purchased BTC to engage in illegal activity have had their accounts unexpectedly closed.

Online exchanges usually have a wallet associated with them. When you buy bitcoin, the BTC goes into your wallet at the exchange and stays there until you move it somewhere else.

NEVER LEAVE YOUR BTC IN AN EXCHANGE'S WALLET! Once your purchase is complete, move the BTC to a wallet you control. The only exception is if you are engaged in day trading or arbitrage but you are a new user and will not be doing either of those things.

Remember that exchanges are not banks. Exchanges have been hacked, have "lost" Bitcoin, and have scammed users and have also gone bankrupt through their own incompetence/malfeasance. When an exchange is in trouble, one of the first things they do is block the withdrawal of BTC from their online wallets. The lesson of "MtGox" is a great reminder of why you should never leave money on an exchange.

**Your bank does not like Bitcoin**. There are documented cases of people who have had their transactions blocked or their accounts at major banks closed due to "suspicious activity" after sending money to an exchange. It didn't happen often and has not happened recently but it has happened and will certainly happen again.

Online Exchanges can also slow when demand spikes. Their websites may become unavailable, or purchases and transactions may take a long time to complete. Unexplained cancellations of purchases are not unheard of.

# 11 EXCHANGING BITCOIN.

**In-Person exchange.** If you live in an area with a lot of Bitcoin users, you may be able to meet someone and conduct a cash dollar-to-BTC transaction. Services such as Localbitcoins (localbitcoins.com) and Mycelium Marketplace (via the Mycelium Wallet on Android) can connect buyers and sellers. This method is more private and potentially faster than using an exchange, but prices will be higher. There is also the matter of security. Follow the rules of meeting a date you met online by conducting the transaction in a public, well-lit place, as you will be meeting an unknown person who knows you are carrying cash.

**Bitcoin ATMs.** There are Bitcoin ATMs and no, there is probably not one near you. But they do exist, and you can use Google or CoinATMRadar to find one. CoinATMRadar also has an app you can load on your smartphone for mobile use. There are several types of ATM, and the exact procedure for using them varies. Be prepared to provide identification.

**Other Bitcoin Wallets.** Some Bitcoin wallets like Mycelium have partnered with exchanges to provide the ability to buy and sell BTC from within the wallet itself, often using a credit/debit card. These are essentially just links to online exchanges. Expect to pay more for the convenience.

Services like BitQuick (www.bitquick.com) operate like a cross between a local bitcoin broker and a regular exchange. They connect buyers and sellers, but instead of meeting online, the exchange happens remotely, with the buyer depositing cash directly into the seller's bank account. There is usually some form of escrow involved to ensure no one gets cheated.

# 12 HOW NOT TO OBTAIN BITCOIN!

Bitcoin Faucets. These are websites that will send you very small amounts of BTC in exchange for you just visiting their page which is full of advertisements. There is nothing wrong or illegal about faucets, but people new to Bitcoin tend to get the wrong idea about how much they can get this way. Faucets provide EXTREMELY small amounts (fractions of a cent), and you typically have to wait until you amass a minimum amount before they will send you your BTC. Unless you have a lot of patience and a high tolerance for frustration and advertising skip the faucets.

Scams, schemes, and "investments". Bitcoin's history is filled with "investments" that paid interest or dividends in BTC. Not all of them have been outright scams, but the vast majority were. Most of these were easy to identify as scams due to their wild claims of guaranteed results for little or no risk. Some made more believable claims yet still vanished suddenly or were shut down. If someone offers to pay you bitcoin dividends if you deposit your BTC with them or buy "stock" in their Bitcoin venture, run. Assume they are a scam, even if their numbers seem to add up. You will be right far more often than wrong.

# 13 INVESTING IN BITCOIN.

Whether purchasing a large amount of BTC and hoping you can sell it for a massive profit later (speculating) or buying and selling BTC to take profit from short-term price fluctuations (trading), is it worth the risk?

**People made A LOT of money investing in Bitcoin.** In early 2011, one BTC was worth $1 USD. Today, in 2017, one BTC is $2100. If you had invested in BTC when it was below one dollar, you would have amassed a life-changing amount of money in less than a decade. Some of the early winners were developers or savvy hobbyists who saw the potential in Bitcoin and made a decision that turned out to be a wildly profitable. Others were folks who heard about Bitcoin and, knowing little more about it beyond where to buy some, bought a bunch because other people were doing it. The first group of people was investors who knew what they were doing and took a calculated risk. The second group was gamblers who got lucky.

Bitcoin has made millionaires.

It has also ruined people. The rise from cents to thousands of dollars was not a straight line. From late 2013 to early 2014, BTC experienced a drop from over $1200 to around $350. It did not return to the $1200 level until

March of 2017. People who bought in at the top and sold in frustration when the price dropped lost a lot of money. At one point in 2014, the top post on the popular Bitcoin forum on Reddit was a link to a suicide hotline. It was not a joke.

Investment advice: Do not invest in things you don't understand and maybe even more importantly, do not invest money you can't afford to lose.

If you are a new speculator or trader, Bitcoin is not a place for you to learn.

I do not believe Bitcoin has exhausted its upward potential. There is still profit to be made in the long term, but only by those who tread carefully and put in the effort to learn what they're investing in. What I do recommend for Bitcoin newbies is to learn the process of obtaining, spending, and securely storing Bitcoin by actually doing it yourself.

In the beginning, instead of money, invest your time time and energy. See how Bitcoin works. Observe what problems Bitcoin solves and what problems it still has to overcome before it can achieve mass adoption. Participate in discussions in online forums like Reddit or bitcoin websites. Dive deep and It will not take long for you to appreciate Bitcoin's potential and its weaknesses, enabling you to make wiser investment decisions.

# 14 BITCOIN SECURITY.

True security can only be declared after a long history of successful resistance to attack. This is as true for currencies as national borders, medieval castles or my liver. Bitcoin has been tested/ attacked constantly since it first hit the internet in 2008. The Bitcoin network has survived these attacks and grown more resistant to them as developers fix bugs and address weaknesses.

Also remember that Bitcoin is as secure as your computer!

Most people are comfortable using bitcoin to purchase items online or in person. Bitcoin is "secure enough" the most you would likely lose in the event of some unforeseen issue is the equivalent of the good or service you just tried to purchase. The merchants exposure is much higher. A merchant may deal with thousands to tens of thousands of dollars in bitcoin.

You must decide for yourself whether Bitcoin is "secure enough" for whatever you are trying to do. A large and growing number of people consider Bitcoin to be more secure than credit cards for online transactions but would not yet use it as long-term storage for large sums of wealth.

# 15 POSSIBLE THREATS.

- Hackers stealing your money or using your personal information to ruin your credit.
- A software or network glitch that causes BTC to "vanish" from your wallet.
- A government or corporation blocking access to your funds.
- Fluctuations in exchange rates due to demand in other countries.

Evaluating Bitcoin's security against every potential threat is next to impossible, so it is important to decide which threats are your major concern.

While no software or network is 100% unbreakable, the nature of Bitcoin and the Blockchain makes this super unlikely. I have close to zero concern about this threat. The Bitcoin Protocol is about as safe as it can be. The idea of a software glitch that wipes your money is even less of a concern than hackers because every Bitcoin transaction has a permanent record in a public, distributed ledger. A mistake in the Bitcoin protocol cannot change that ledger. A bug in your wallet software cannot go back in time and make your deposits disappear.

Any worry should involve the security of your computer or the specific wallet software you're using.

**What about price volatility and Inflation?** The value of a US Dollar decreases over time due to inflation, but so far has not seen significant inflation from one day to the next.

The value of bitcoin has experienced some exciting rises and drops in its history, some of which took place over days or weeks. The long-term price trend, however, is upward. What does all this mean? It means that your bitcoin is 100% secure from inflation but is very vulnerable to price volatility. If you are using Bitcoin as a way to store money over the long term, then the lack of inflation and the upward price trend work in your favor. If you are using Bitcoin to buy and sell things, then both inflation and price volatility are irrelevant. Your time frame is probably too short for either of them to matter. If you are somewhere in between, however, things can get scary. If you are saving bitcoin for something you will need soon, but not right away, you might get bitten by some unexpected price volatility. Bitcoin is not a good way to store money for your vacation in a few months. In 2010 a developer bought 2 pizzas for 10,000 BTC. Just a few years later, that amount of BTC would be worth 100 million dollars. The price of pizza on the other hand has remained relatively stable.

One of the essential trade-offs of using Bitcoin is assuming full responsibility for securing your own wealth. There are a lot of people who can offer you advice and assistance, but the responsibility and liability is all on you. Remember those banks and payment processors that Bitcoin is trying to make optional? Most credit cards do not hold you liable for charges if your account is compromised. If a bank folds and takes your money with it, the FDIC insures you for up to $100,000. Neither of those is true for Bitcoin. If you remove the 3rd parties, you remove the protections that they offer.

**Are you ready for that responsibility?** Recall that bitcoin is stored in addresses, and you need a Bitcoin wallet to perform transactions with those addresses. The Bitcoin wallet is software that runs on your computer or your smartphone. Instead of being concerned about whether Bitcoin is secure, you should ask yourself some questions about your own security:

- Does your smartphone have a strong password?
- Do you ever install apps from sources other than the App Store or Play Store?
- How strong is your computer's password?
- Do you keep the operating system updated?
- Do you keep the other software that you run updated?
- Do you run cracked copies of games or software?
- Does your computer have a virus or trojan?
- How certain are you?

None of the above questions are specific to Bitcoin. People perform electronic banking functions on their phones and computers all the time, and the same precautions apply to them. The difference is that with banking, your bank will not hold you 100% accountable if a hacker uses your computer to empty your account. Bitcoin isn't like a bank account, Bitcoin is like cash. No limited liability. No deposit insurance. If someone steals the cash out of your purse that cash is gone. If someone gets access to your Bitcoin wallet, your bitcoin becomes their bitcoin. This does not mean that Bitcoin was hacked... it means that YOU were hacked. It wasn't Bitcoin's job to prevent that. It was yours.

Some are not ready for that level of responsibility for large fractions of their net worth. As a beginner, you should keep your use of Bitcoin at or below your comfort level until you educate yourself in both computer and Bitcoin security.

Some tips about remaining secure:

- **Never reuse an address if you can avoid it.** A Bitcoin address should only be used to receive funds once.

When you wish to send more BTC to your wallet, send it to a new address in your wallet. (NOTE: An exception to this is cold or "paper" wallets, which is described below.

- **Set a passcode.** Your phone and computer should have a passcode and/or password. If your Bitcoin wallet supports setting its own separate PIN number or passcode, do it. This makes it a little slower to access your BTC, but the extra security is worth the slight inconvenience.
- **Back up your wallet.** Your Bitcoin wallet is more than just a list of addresses. Each address has a unique secret code to access its contents. You'll probably never use those codes directly; the software handles that for you. Another thing the software should do is provide a way to backup those codes and restore them into a new wallet. The exact mechanism for doing this differs, but on smartphones, it usually involves the wallet showing you a long list of random words. Those words are the secret codes transformed into a format that is easier for humans to deal with. You don't need to memorize them. You need to write them down and keep them very, very secure. If your phone gets damaged or stolen, you can type those words into the wallet running on another phone and recover your bitcoin.
- **Do not leave BTC in an online wallet service, such as those offered by** exchanges. Your Bitcoin wallet should be on your phone, on your computer, or on a special piece of hardware you've acquired for that purpose (see below). It should never be "in the cloud". If a website offers to keep your BTC for you, do NOT take them up on that offer. Even if the website is someone you trust with other things (such as an exchange where you buy BTC), letting anyone else control access to your BTC is a REALLY BAD IDEA. The only exception is traders who are buying/selling BTC for profit. In addition to losing money in a bad trade, one of the risks traders assume is that of losing money due to an exchange

hack, malice or incompetence. Non-traders need not expose themselves to these risks, so don't.

- **Do not keep large sums of money in a computer or phone-based wallet.** The definition of "large sum" varies with the individual, but you should treat a Bitcoin wallet like a physical wallet. If you don't walk around with your entire net worth in cash in your pocket, don't do it with Bitcoin. Instead, use hardware, paper, or offline wallets for large sums and/or long-term storage.

An offline wallet is a wallet on a machine which you leave offline and use for only one purpose: to store and transfer BTC. It is not used to surf the web. It is not used to play games. It is not used to check email. It is dedicated to Bitcoin and nothing else. Real-world examples may be an old smartphone or laptop you've wiped (factory reset), installed Bitcoin software on, and then disconnected from the internet. Even without a network connection, the addresses in these wallets can still receive bitcoin. You just can't make new transactions to spend the BTC without taking the machine online. Since the machine is not online, some virus or random hacker on the internet can't steal your bitcoin.

If you need something more secure and robust than an old phone, you can purchase a specialized piece of hardware such as a Trezor. This hardware wallet allows you to use any PC for BTC transactions, even if the PC is compromised. It is beyond the needs of a new user, but if you find yourself amassing a large quantity of BTC you may need to graduate to something like this. For now, just remember that these things exist.

My favorite method of offline storage is a paper wallet. A paper wallet is a piece of paper, plastic or metal, with a Bitcoin address written on it, along with the secret code used to access the BTC. Recall from above that an address does not need to be online to receive bitcoin. You can send bitcoin to the address without fear that its associated computer will be hacked because there is no associated computer. In this way, it is similar to the offline wallets discussed above, but with no spare machine, to keep offline. When you need to spend the funds, most Bitcoin wallets will allow you to import the paper wallet address, using the secret code and transfer its contents. This takes only a few seconds and is a lot less complicated than it sounds. I cannot overstate the need to protect the paper wallet from theft or destruction.

Also, obtaining a paper wallet is not as straightforward as using one. I do not recommend ordering them online, as you are trusting the creator not to record the secret codes before mailing them to you. There are websites like Bitaddress.org and walletgenerator.net that allow you to generate and print them yourself, but once again you are trusting the website not to secretly record the codes. The best method is to download the creation software yourself, run it on your PC and print the resulting addresses and codes to a printer physically connected to your computer. As with hardware wallets, a paper wallet is not something a new user needs to worry about; just remember they are an option.

- **Do NOT use a Brain Wallet.** A brain wallet is a paper wallet without the paper. The secret codes I've mentioned above are long strings of random letters and numbers impossible for the average person to remember or guess. But what if you COULD remember one? In that case, you would have a Bitcoin address you could access by typing the random gibberish into some wallet software. So now what if someone made a Bitcoin address whose secret code was something easy to remember? Then they would have a brain wallet. Unfortunately, things that are easy to remember like quotes, song lyrics, or passages from books are also easy for computers to guess. If you created a brain wallet with an easy-to-remember secret code and sent BTC to it, there is a near 100% chance that someone has ALREADY guessed it and imported it into their wallet. Their computers are now watching YOUR address, waiting to steal whatever money you send to it.

**Bitcoin is not Anonymous.** However, with sufficient effort, you can make it extremely difficult to tie your Bitcoin transactions to your identity.

Note that "extremely difficult" and "impossible" are not the same thing.

The public ledger contains a record of every Bitcoin transaction. The ledger is viewable by anyone. Recall that the ledger doesn't contain names or identifying information associated with the transactions. All you will see are addresses, timestamps, and amounts. Specifically, you will see the addresses from which the bitcoins in the transaction originated (sources) and the addresses where they were sent (destinations). If you looked at one of those source or destination addresses you will see more transactions with still more addresses. You can trace the bitcoin forward and backward in time to either their current address or the address where they were generated.

But if none of this information contains a name, address, or social security number, doesn't that mean everything is anonymous? No. A sufficiently motivated person can discover enough trace information to unmask your identity and/or the identities of those you transact with. If at any point your bitcoins touch an entity that knows your real-world identity (such as an employer or a Bitcoin exchange), then your identity can be divulged with a subpoena (or other means), and then your transactions can be traced across the ledger with your name now attached to them.

So how does one go about making their identity harder to obtain? The simplest way is to never use the same Bitcoin address twice. Instead, use your wallet software to generate a new recipient address for every transaction in which you are receiving BTC.

You can also avoid buying or selling Bitcoin on an exchange, and instead purchase your BTC with in-person transactions.

To take privacy to the next level, use a mixer or tumbler service to obfuscate the source of your bitcoin. Tumblers create a series of transactions among multiple users. At the end, each user gets back the same amount of BTC that they put in but they do not receive the exact same coins. Think of it like this: Someone has recorded the serial numbers of all the dollar bills you own to track your spending. You and three strangers put all the cash you have into a shoe box. You shake the box and then withdraw the same amount of cash you dropped in. You have just as much money as you had before, but you don't have the exact same bills. Whoever was tracking you would have to find a way to associate your identity with your NEW dollar bills, as the old association is no longer valid.

Don't worry if this sounds complicated or unnecessary because for the average new Bitcoin user, tumbling and mixing is unnecessary.

# 16 CHALLENGES FOR BITCOINS LONGEVITY AND MAINSTREAM APPEAL.

**Capacity.** Under the current architecture, Bitcoin has a limited capacity for the number of transactions it can handle per hour. Recall that transactions are written to the public ledger in blocks, and a block is written every 10 minutes on average. There is also a limit on the size of a block. This restricts the number of transactions that the network can handle per hour. This was not a problem when Bitcoin was small and relatively unknown, but as Bitcoin moved out of the realm of hobbyists and into the mainstream, the system's capacity became a growth-limiting obstacle that still needs to be addressed.

Some want to increase the maximum size of the blocks. Some want to alter the way the protocol functions so that transactions can be smaller and more of them can fit into blocks. Still others want to take no action and let the free market or the "fee market" in this case, do its job. The details of these potential solutions are beyond this introductory text, but until some solution is reached, users should expect increasing fees and/or longer wait times as the backlog of unwritten transactions grows.

**Increasing Fees.** One of the original selling points of Bitcoin was the low cost of transferring funds, regardless of distance or amount. This still holds true to a large degree, however, the fees required to transact in BTC have risen considerably. While years ago, it may have cost one cent to send a transaction, today that same transaction may cost you $1.15. While the transaction fees are still much lower than competing traditional systems such as Western Union, they eat away at Bitcoin's suitability for sending small amounts or buying low-cost items. Spending $1 to send $3 to someone is goofy. Fees will fall when a solution to the capacity limit is implemented. But fee increase due to exchange rate will continue as long as bitcoin increases in value.

**Merchant Acceptance.** The number of merchants that accept BTC is still a small percentage of those that accept traditional payment methods like credit cards. However, there has been tremendous growth in recent years, and that growth is not slowing. Companies like Gyft allow you to use bitcoin to purchase gift cards and Purse.io enables you to purchase items from Amazon with BTC. The limited acceptance of Bitcoin is less of an issue each year.

**Public Perception.** Bitcoin has been accused of being a Ponzi scheme, a tool of terrorists, drug dealers and/or pedophiles, being 'dead' or otherwise doomed to imminent failure, a government conspiracy... the list is long. And yet, Bitcoin continues to not only exist but prosper. People resist change, and Bitcoin represents a massive change in the financial industry. It is not just a tool that could make the current financial infrastructure more efficient, it can make large parts of that infrastructure irrelevant. To say a certain amount of resistance and name-calling should be expected is an understatement. People tend not to like things they don't understand, and Bitcoin is very complex. The community of developers, enthusiasts, and entrepreneurs that have brought Bitcoin from the hobbyist fringe to the verge of mainstream acceptance must continue to push public awareness and positive perception. If the public views Bitcoin as magical, internet, fairy money for pedophilic terrorist scammers posing as a Prince from Nigeria that uses it to buy heroin from the deep web, they will not adopt it. Plus, unlike other currencies, Bitcoin does not have a government fiat to force people to continue using it. Public perception is a vulnerability that should not be ignored.

**Regulatory Pressures**. When Bitcoin became popular, governments didn't know how to react. They were just as baffled as my parents are now but unlike my parents, the government also wanted to know how to tax it because that is what governments do. For the most part, the US Government took a hands-off approach similar to the one they took with the internet as a whole. Laws needed to be obeyed and taxes needed to be paid as with anything else, but regulating Bitcoin itself was not on their agenda. Some state governments took a more heavy-handed approach. New York, for instance, made it mandatory that Bitcoin companies go through the arduous process of getting a money transmitter license before conducting business. Several companies either shut down or relocated because of that law. Since then, several other states have enacted similar requirements, thus impeding the grown of the Bitcoin economy. The good news is that the actual use of Bitcoin by end-users is unaffected by these laws. Federal and State tax law still treats BTC as a commodity, forcing users to calculate capital gains on every transaction. Regardless of whether you agree with regulation (there are many in the Bitcoin community that do), the real trouble is uncertainty. Governments on any level can change their minds about Bitcoin legality and their regulatory stance toward it at any time. Russia, for instance, banned Bitcoin altogether. Then they decided to un-ban it. This problem is not unique to Bitcoin or Russia. Control is a full time job.

**Complexity.** Bitcoin at first glance is complicated.

## BITCOIN: WHAT ARE THE KIDS UP TO NOW?

Well-designed software with simple user interfaces can mask this complexity from end users, but there will always be a learning curve. The common-sense rules of using Bitcoin are not yet common. Bitcoin may never be as easy to use as cash, but it can be every bit as simple and more secure than a credit card. Plus who wants to touch disgusting cash. Do you know the amount of fecal matter on dollar bills?! Keep your hands clean with Bitcoin.

# 17 SUMMARY

**Final Takeaways:**
- Bitcoin is like cash for the internet.
- The word "bitcoin" can refer to the Bitcoin network, the Bitcoin software, or the bitcoin currency (BTC).
- Bitcoin is legal.
- Bitcoin transactions are irreversible.
- NEVER LEAVE PURCHASED BITCOIN ON AN EXCHANGE!
- Bitcoin is not anonymous but can be very difficult to trace.
- Bitcoin is not free to use, despite what some people might tell you.
- You can purchase bitcoin on exchanges that are required to collect your personal details.
- NEVER LEAVE PURCHASED BITCOIN ON AN EXCHANGE!
- Mining Bitcoin is way too expensive and complicated at this point for beginners.
- Speculating or trading in Bitcoin is not for beginners..
- The weak point in Bitcoin security is your computer or smartphone, not Bitcoin itself.

- The safest way to store BTC long-term is in a paper wallet, hardware wallet, or other offline wallet.
- NEVER LEAVE PURCHASED BITCOIN ON AN EXCHANGE! You have been duly warned.

**Here is a simplified list of steps to get started with Bitcoin:**
- Put a passcode/password on your phone or desktop if you don't already have one.
- Decide on a wallet. Consider Mycelium (Android) or Breadwallet (iOS). Both are free.
- Install the wallet and follow the instructions to backup your wallet. This will probably involve writing down and re-entering random words.
- Go back and follow the instructions to backup your wallet.
- Register at an exchange. There are many. If you don't have time to research for yourself, I recommend using Coinbase or Kraken.
- Satisfy the exchange's KYC ("Know Your Customer") requirements, which may include sending them a picture of your driver's license.
- Use the exchange to purchase BTC with either a bank account or credit card.
- Transfer your BTC to your wallet.
- DO NOT SKIP THE PREVIOUS STEP.

Well, that was a fun ride. Bitcoin and the story of cryptocurrencies is so fluidly dynamic and interesting that I believe it useful for anyone to know at least enough to be able to recognize opportunities in the future. I lacked the basic knowledge when approached by a friend to get into Bitcoin 8 years ago and consequently lost out on a huge financial gain. The gold rush period may well be over, never to return, but having a basic understanding of the possibilities cryptocurrencies offer can better help you to see the next future gold rush in time to capitalize. Gold rushes aside, cryptocurrencies will absolutely play a major part of the democratization of money and therefore power in the future. Why not be a part of the future?!

# ABOUT THE AUTHOR

A traveller always looking for new solutions to old problems, Nathaniel Rollins stumbled into the realm of cryptocurrencies at an Anarcho-Capitalist community in Chile. This is where the Author learned just enough to realize years later about the enormous opportunity he had missed. Nathaniel vowed he would not miss the next opportunity from lack of knowledge and has now learned enough to share with you.

While the new frontiers of tech and ideas are exciting, Nathaniel especially loves the idea of marrying old wisdom and technologies of sustainable living such as Cob Houses, with modern and even future ideas and technology like cryptocurrencies.

www.ingramcontent.com/pod-product-compliance
Lightning Source LLC
Chambersburg PA
CBHW070941220526
45469CB00007B/2474